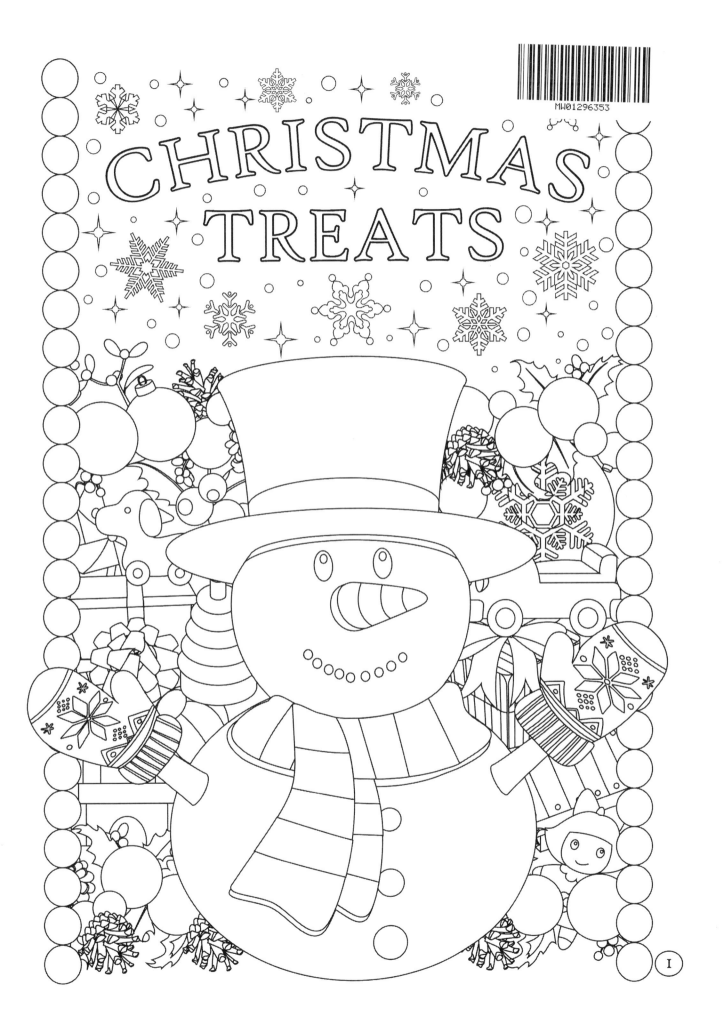

Christmas Treats: A Holiday Coloring Book

Copyright © 2015 SpringMix Media, Inc.

Cover by: Catherine Benante

Illustrations by Catherine Benante and Shutterstock.com

Images are used under license from Shutterstock.com

All rights reserved.

With the exception of photocopying for personal use only, no part of this book may be reproduced in any form by any electronic or mechanical means including photocopying, recording, or information storage and retrieval without permission in writing from the author.

ISBN-13:978-1518673726

ISBN-10:1518673724

www.springmixmedia.com

Printed in U.S.A

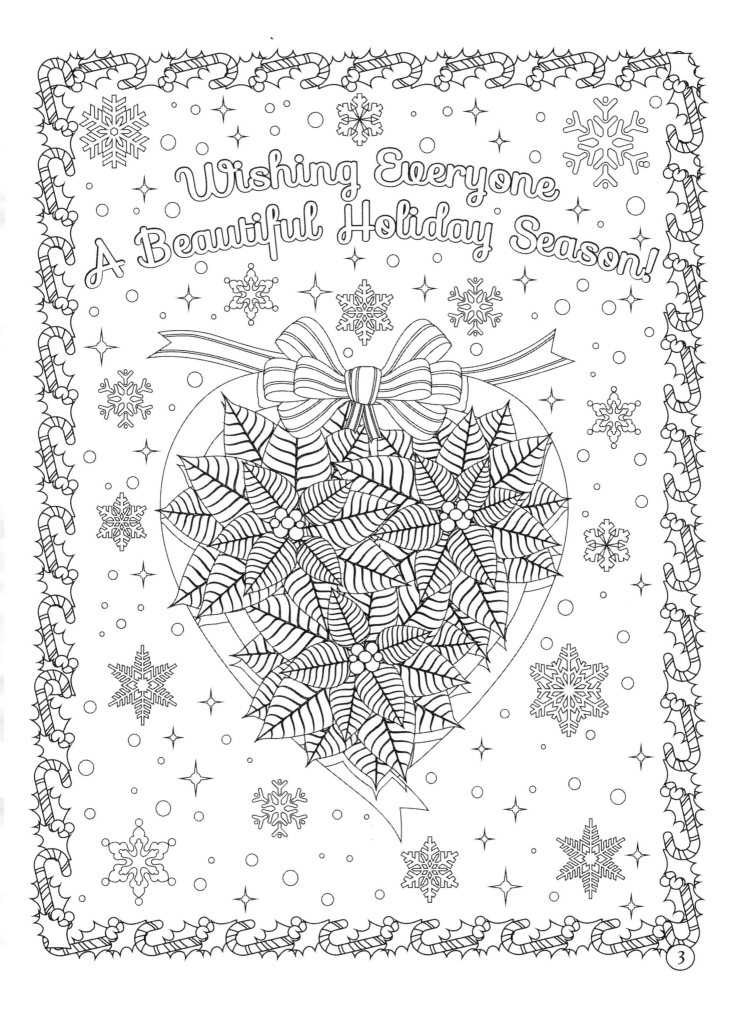

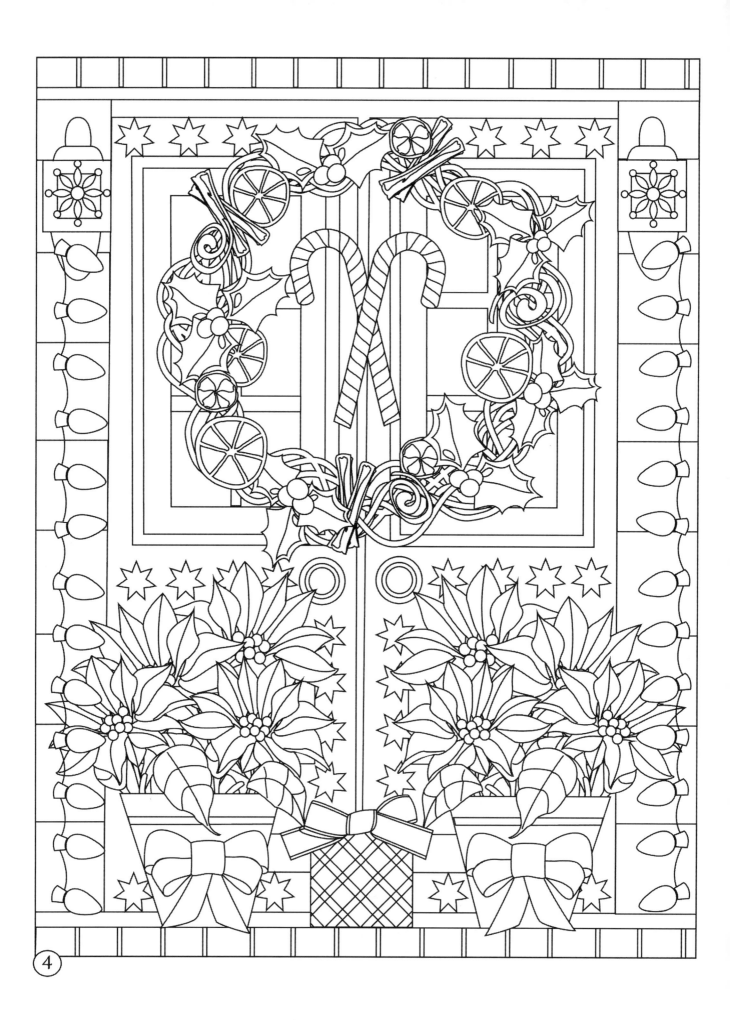

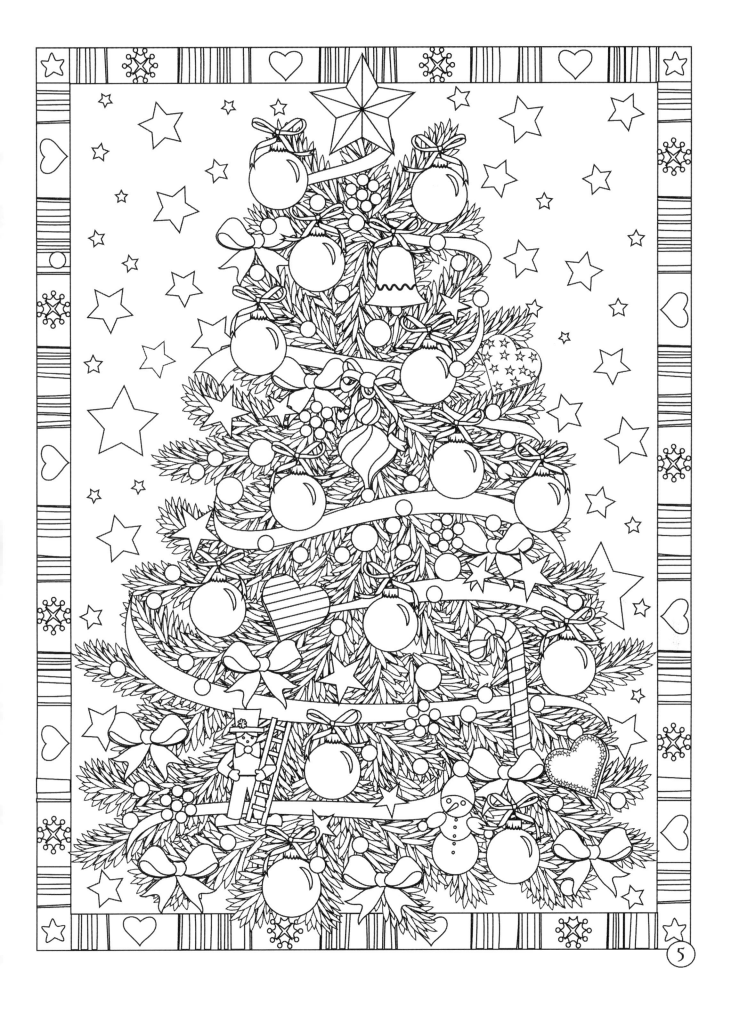

⑥ Blank page - helps avoid marker bleed-through! ☆

Blank page - helps avoid marker bleed-through!

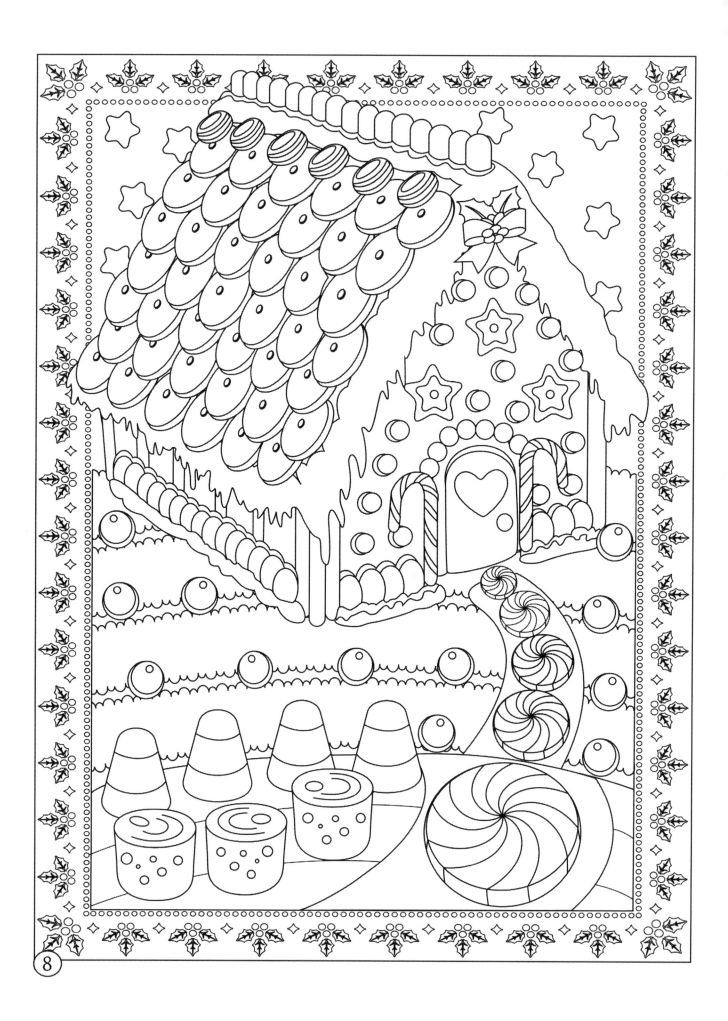

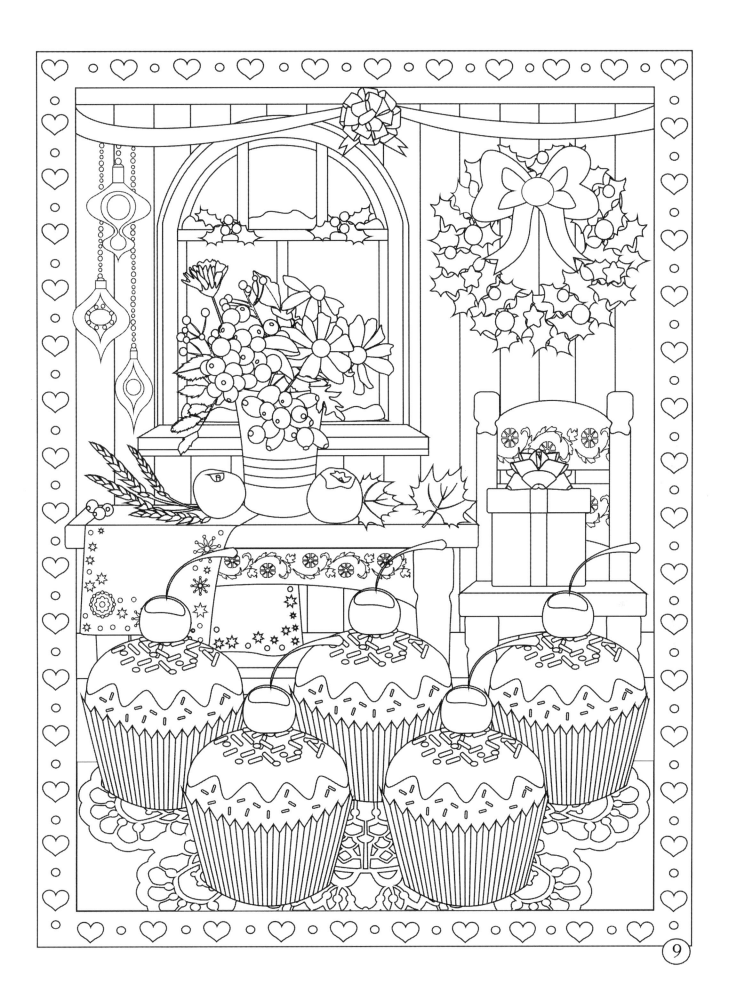

(10) Blank page - helps avoid marker bleed-through!

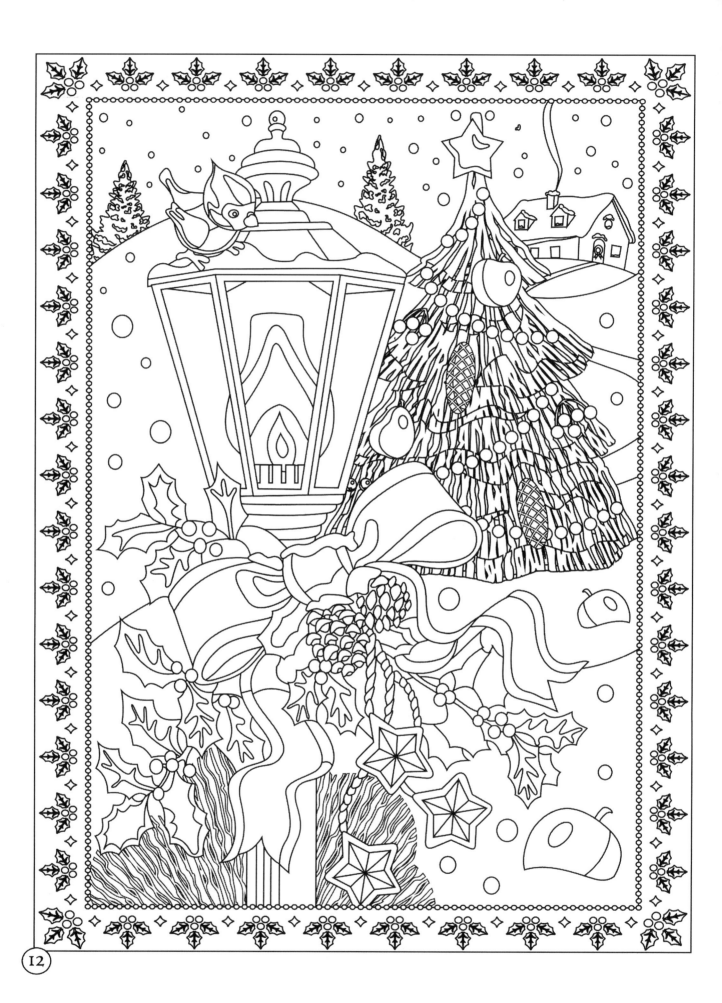

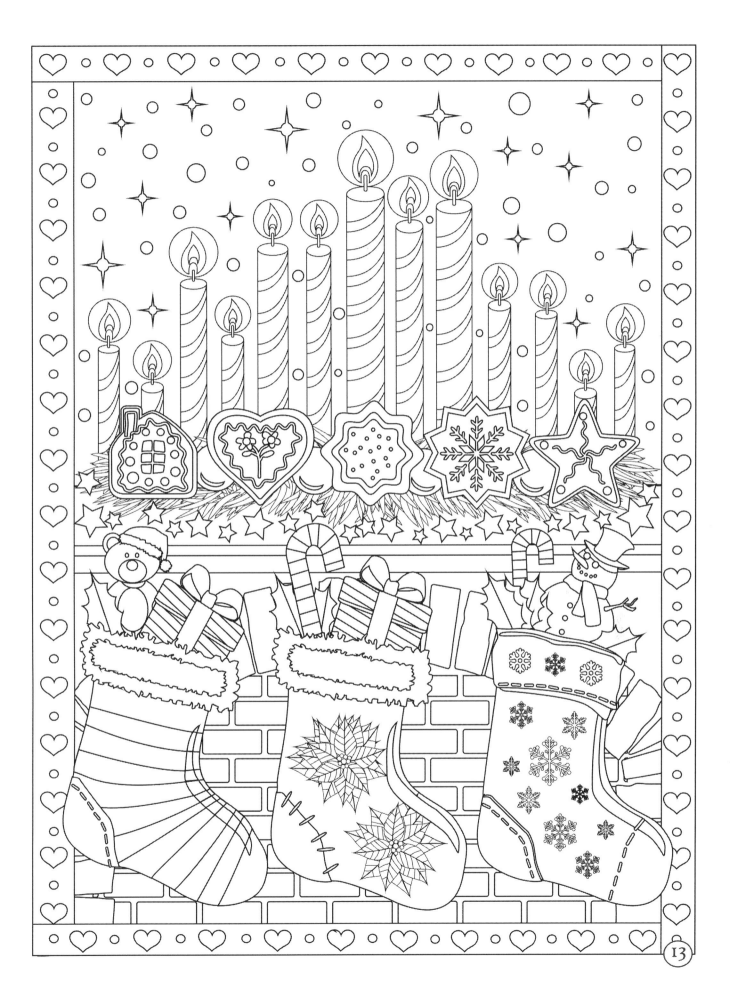

(14) Blank page - helps avoid marker bleed-through! ☆

Blank page - helps avoid marker bleed-through!

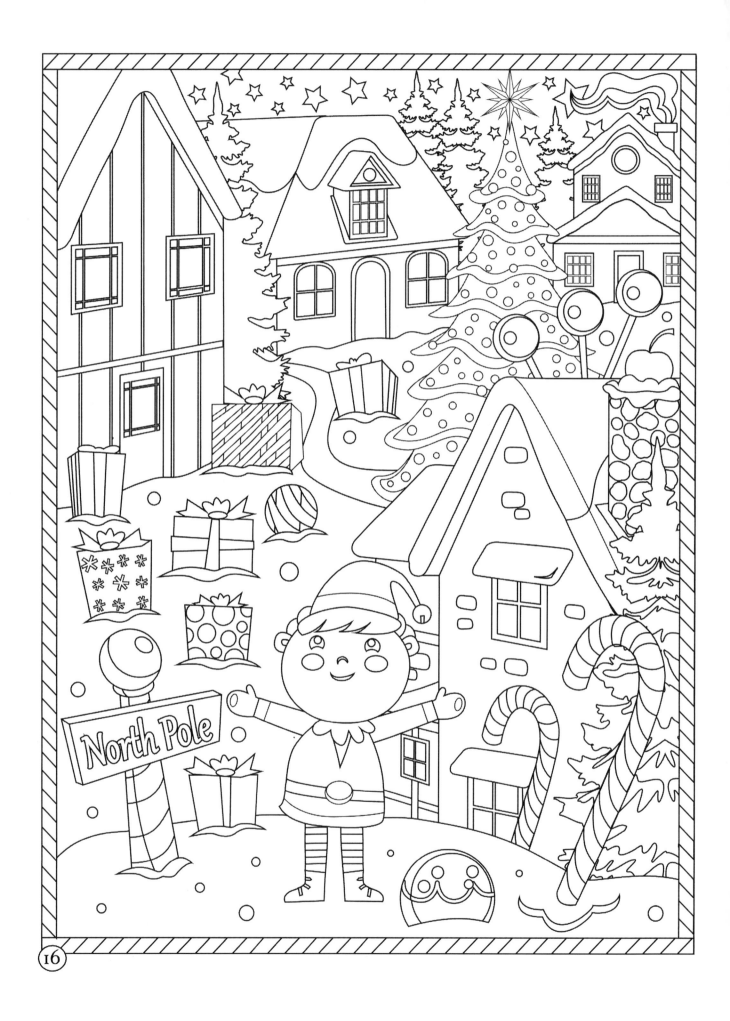

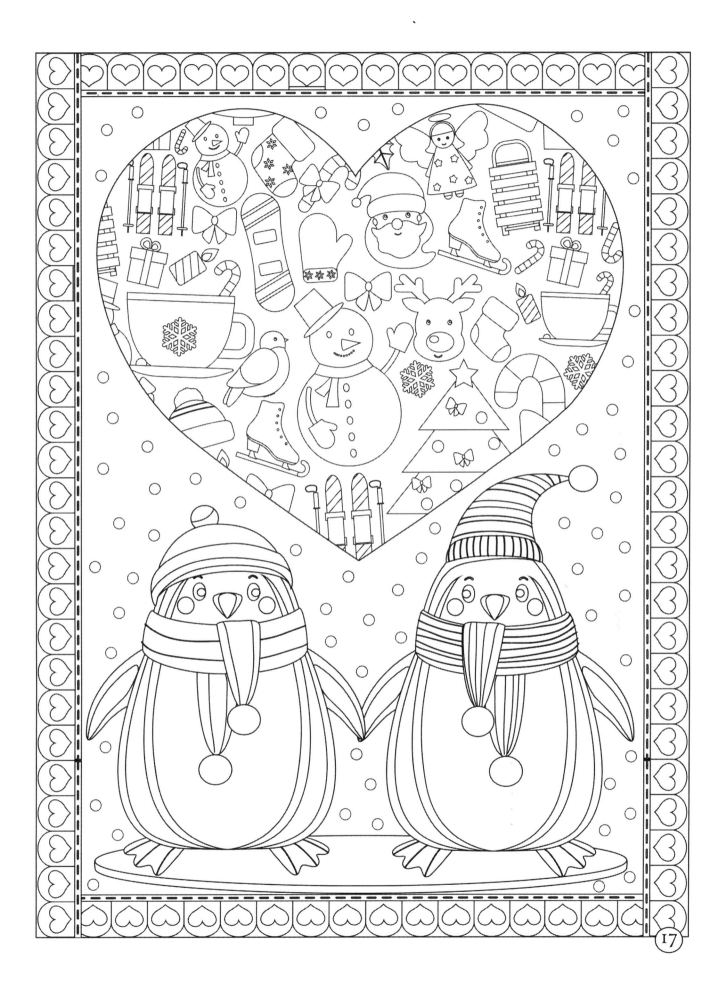

Blank page - helps avoid marker bleed-through!

Blank page - helps avoid marker bleed-through!

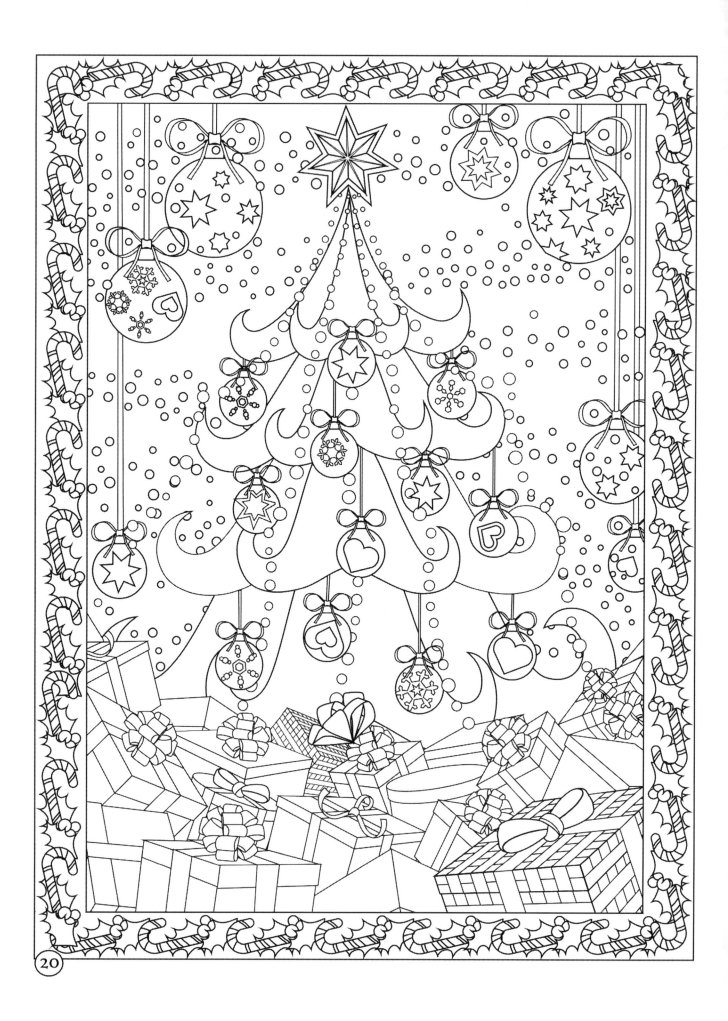

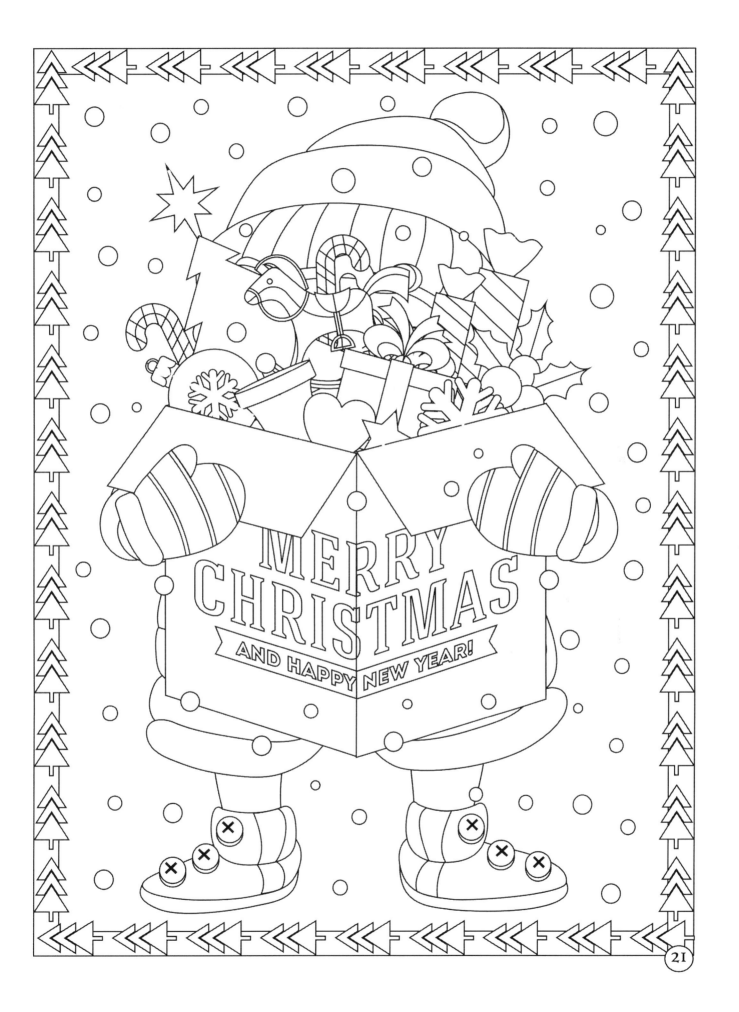

Blank page - helps avoid marker bleed-through!

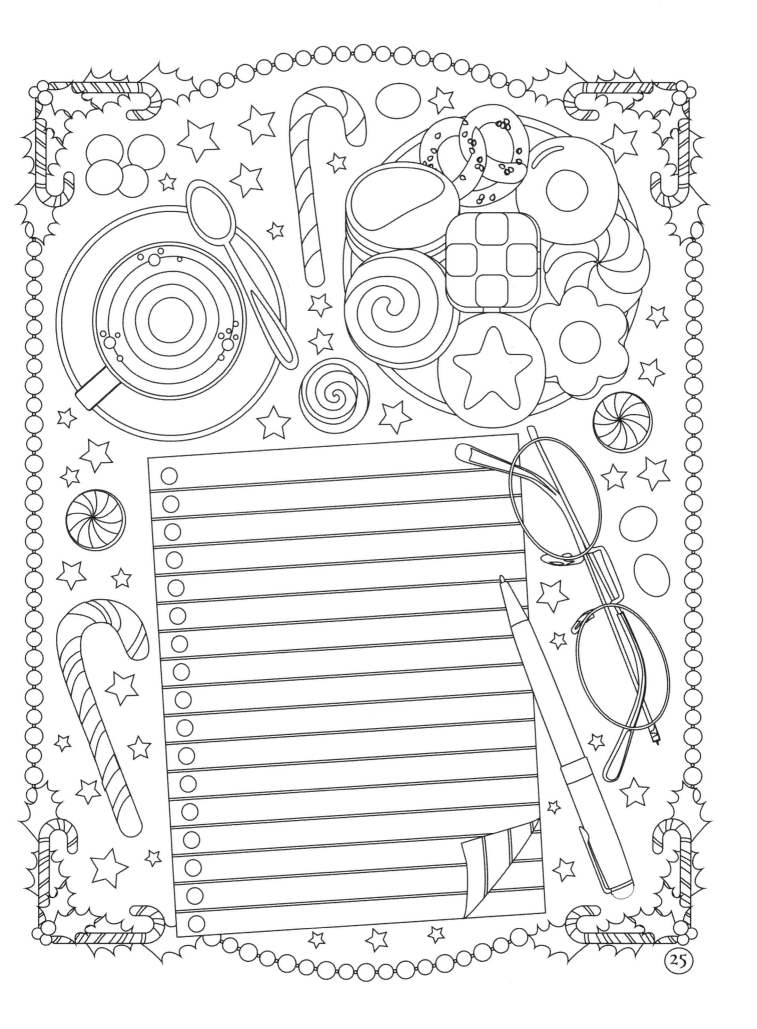

Blank page - helps avoid marker bleed-through!

Blank page - helps avoid marker bleed-through!

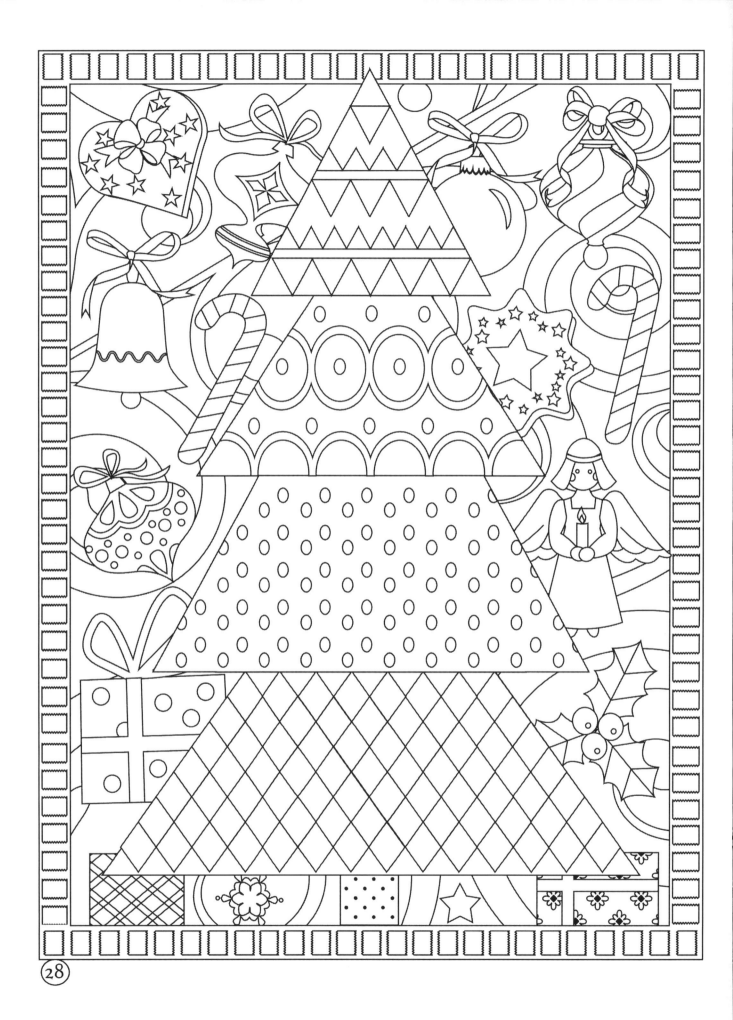

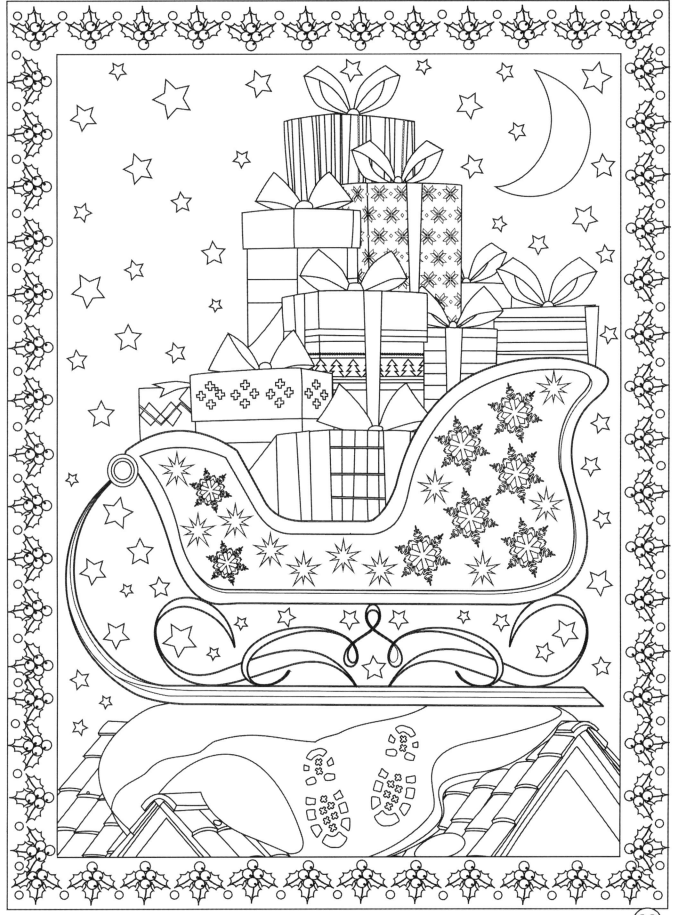

Blank page - helps avoid marker bleed-through!

Blank page - helps avoid marker bleed-through!

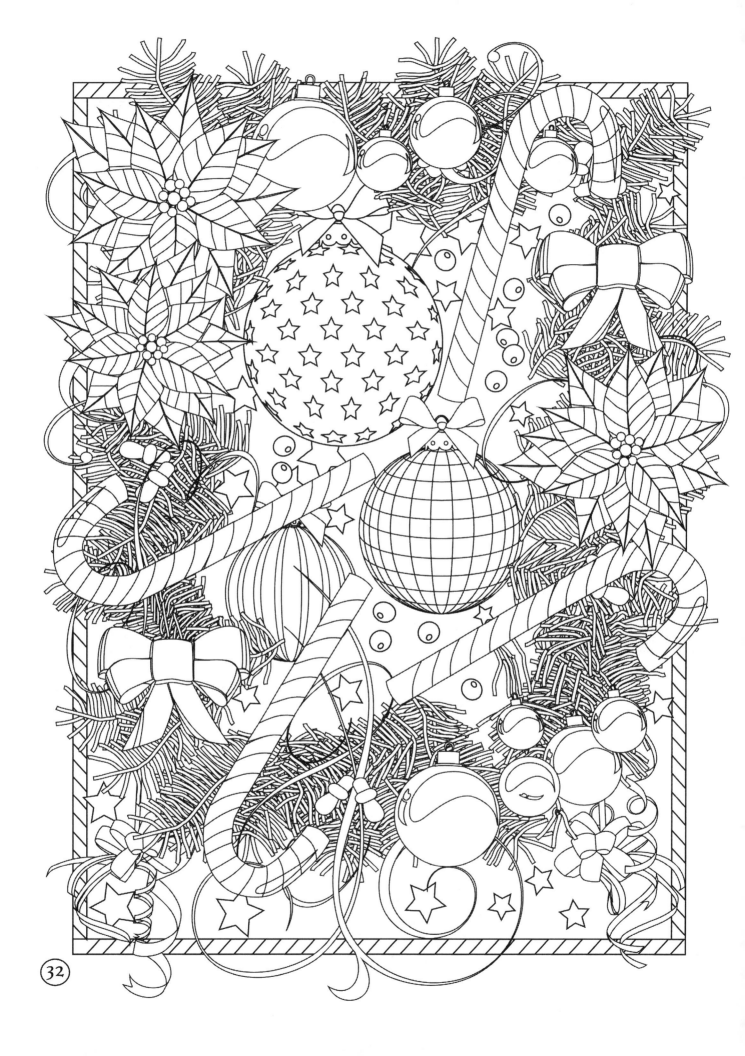

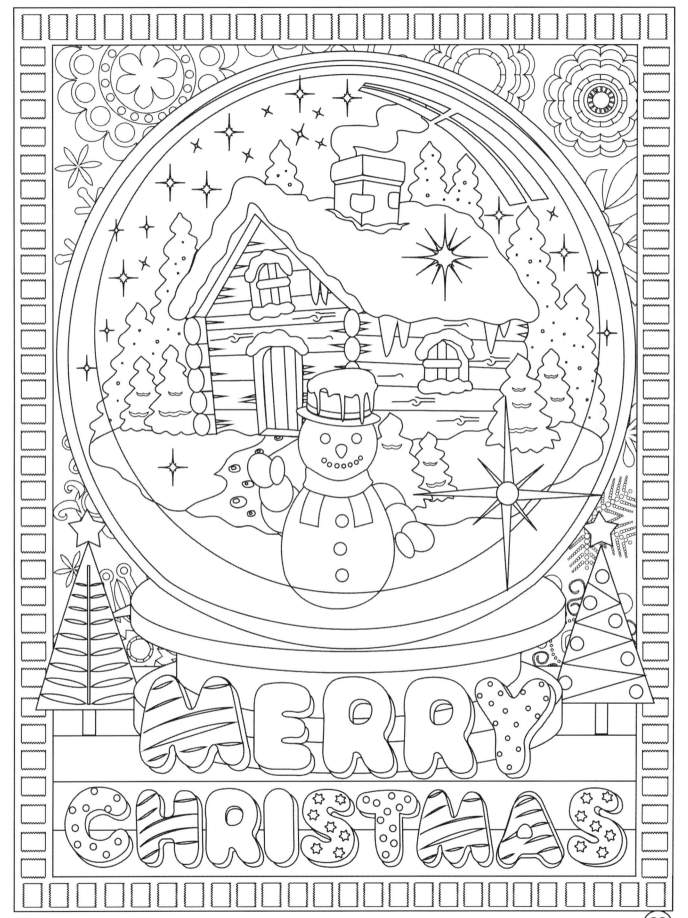

(34) Blank page - helps avoid marker bleed-through!

Blank page - helps avoid marker bleed-through!

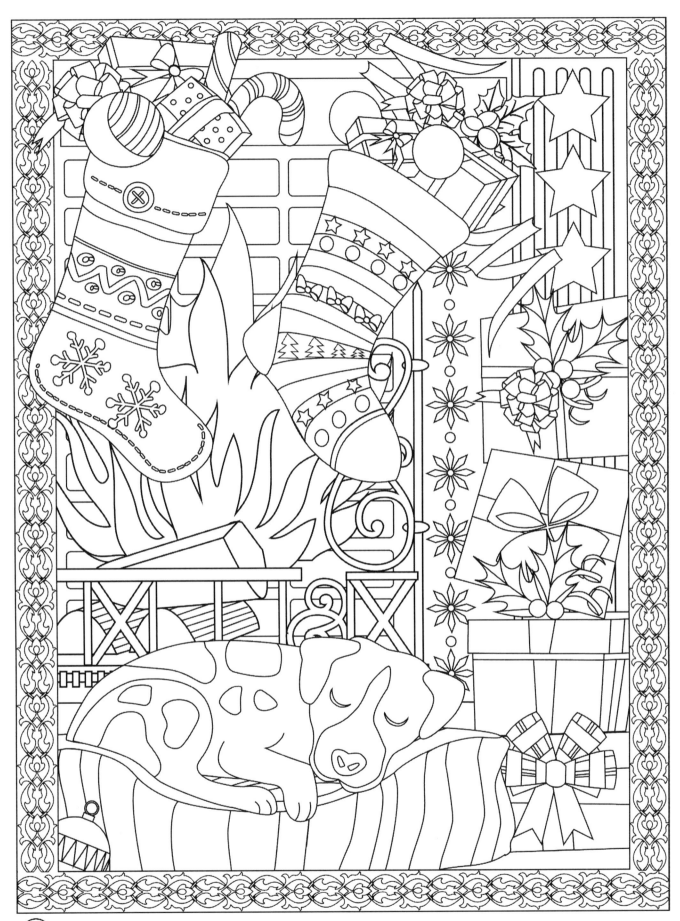

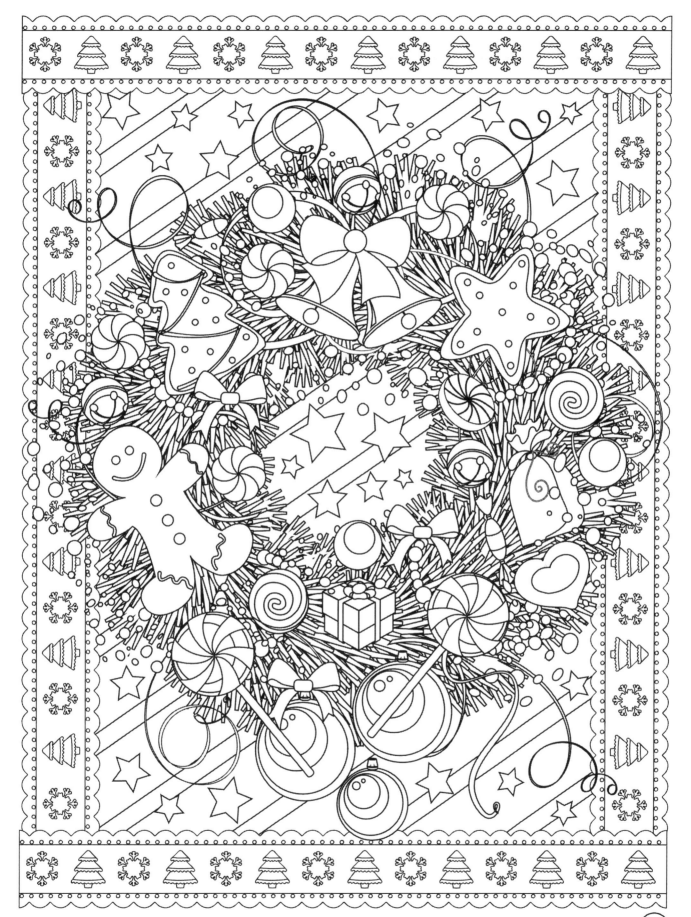

(38) Blank page - helps avoid marker bleed-through!

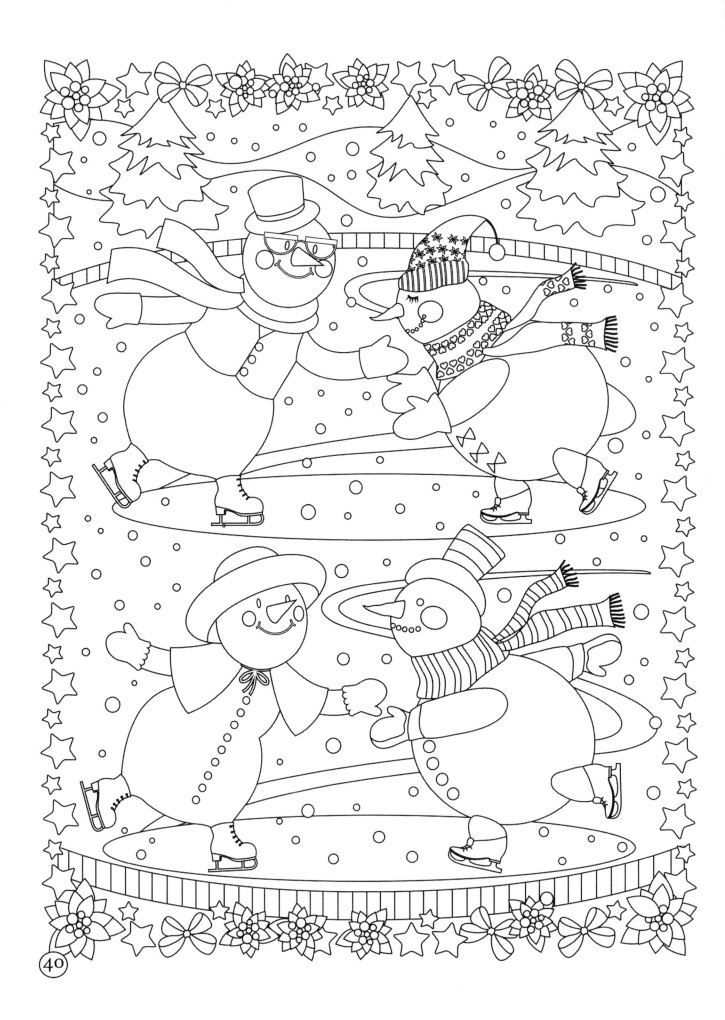

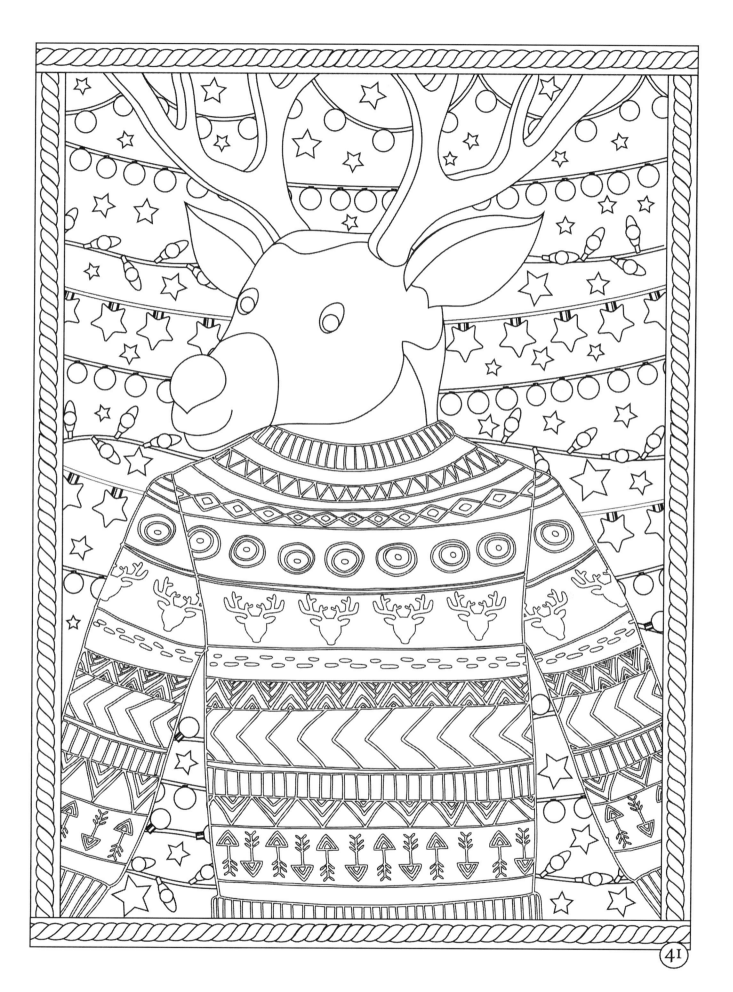

(42) Blank page - helps avoid marker bleed-through! ☆

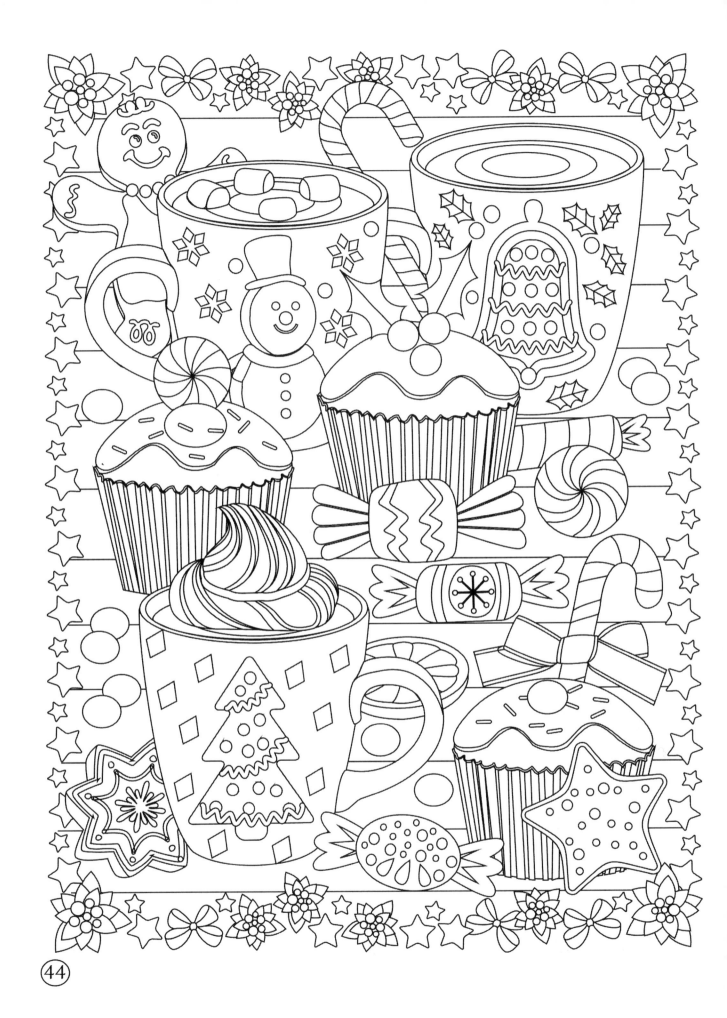

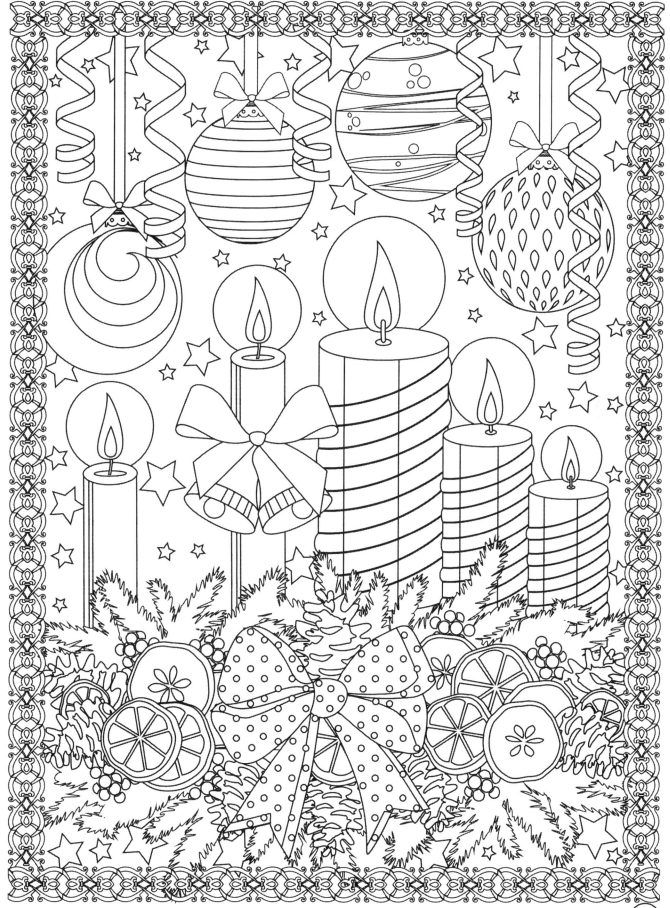

Blank page - helps avoid marker bleed-through!

Blank page - helps avoid marker bleed-through!

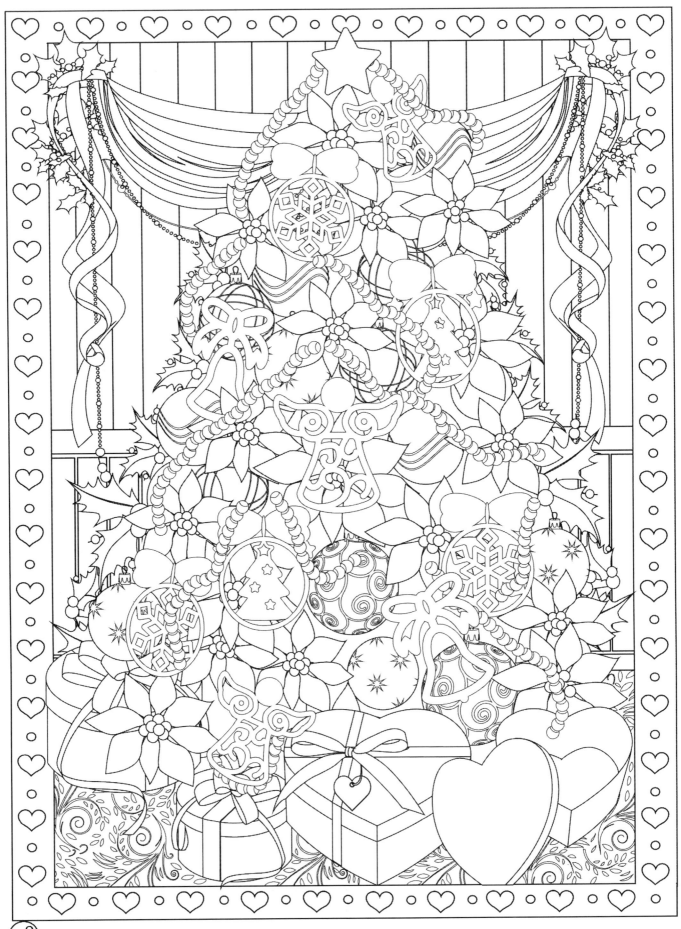

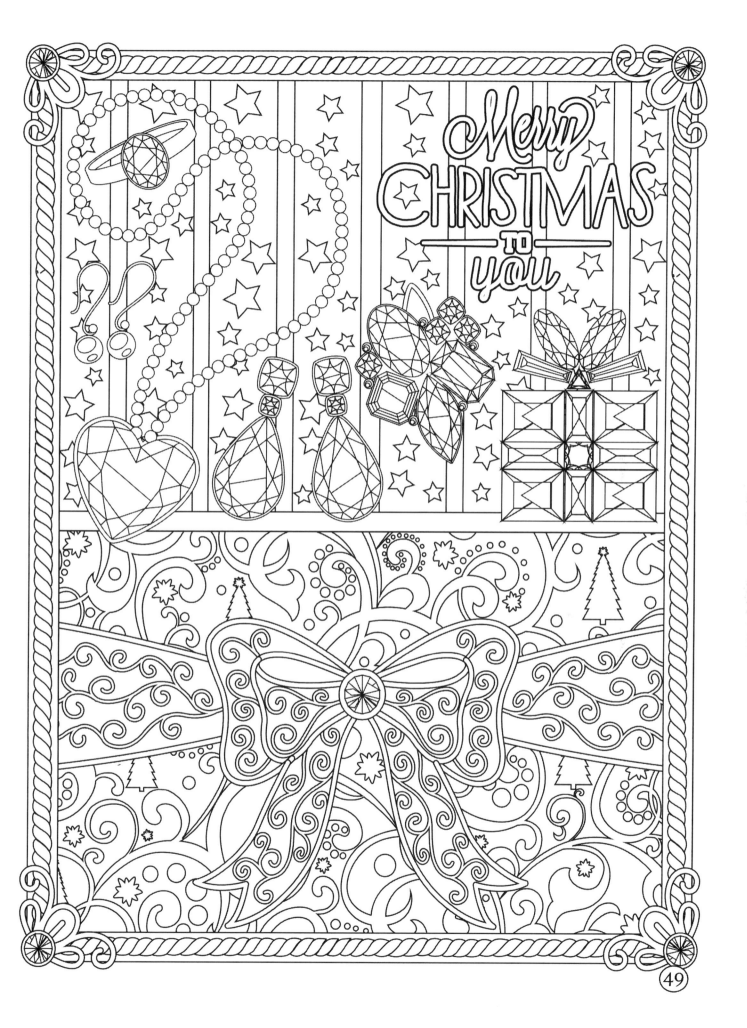

50 Blank page - helps avoid marker bleed-through!

Blank page - helps avoid marker bleed-through!

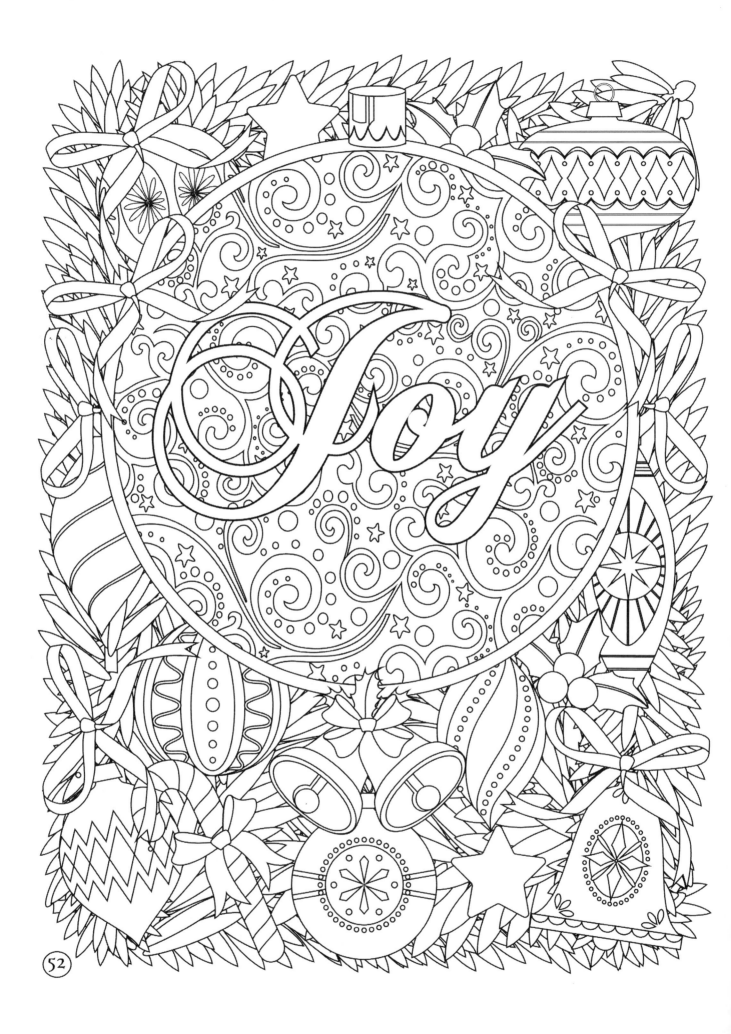

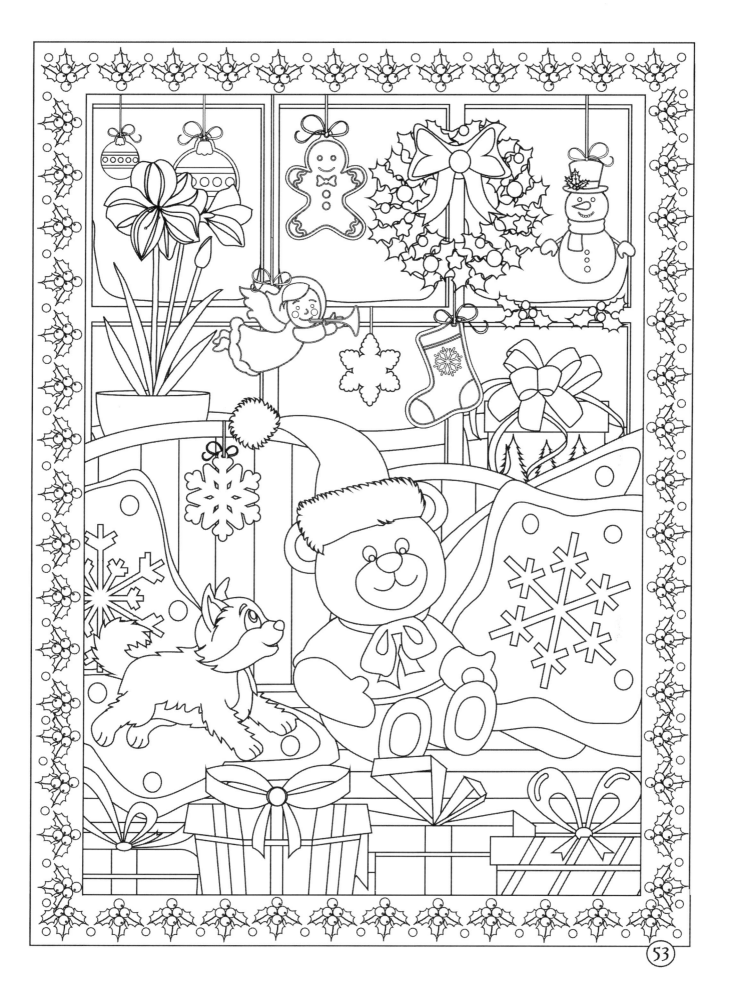

(54) Blank page - helps avoid marker bleed-through! ☆

Blank page - helps avoid marker bleed-through!

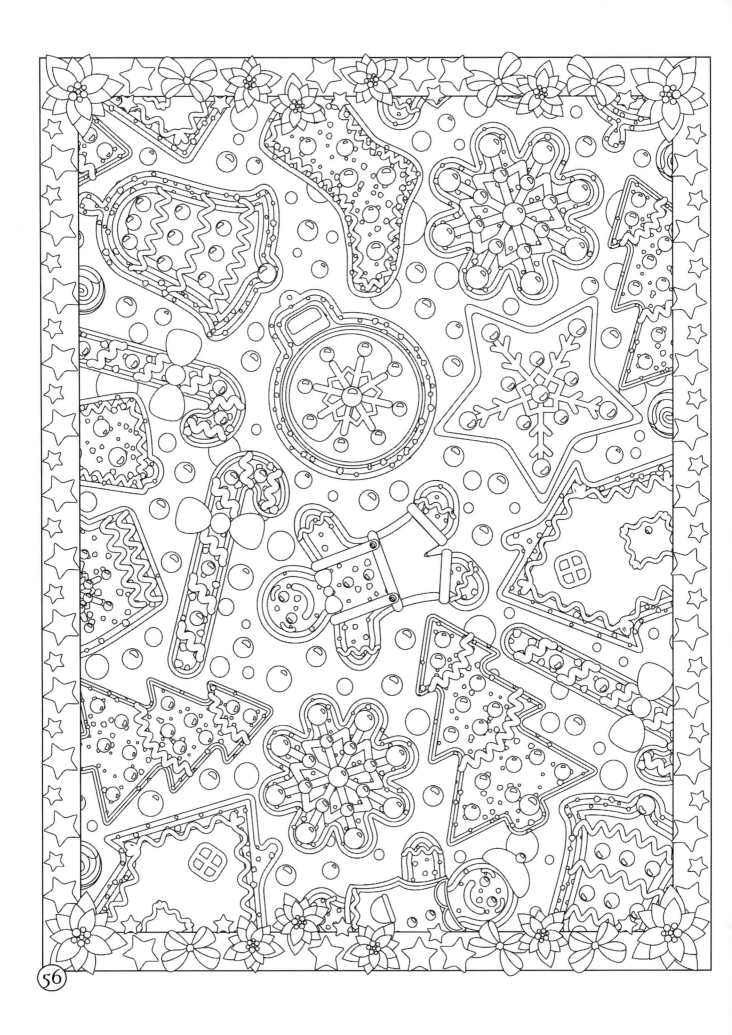

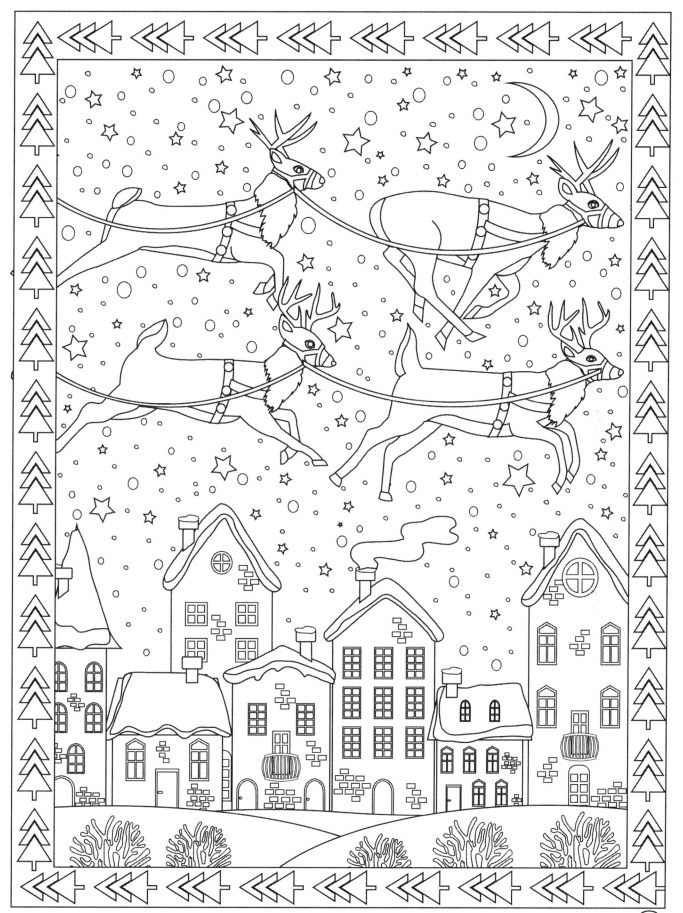

Blank page - helps avoid marker bleed-through!

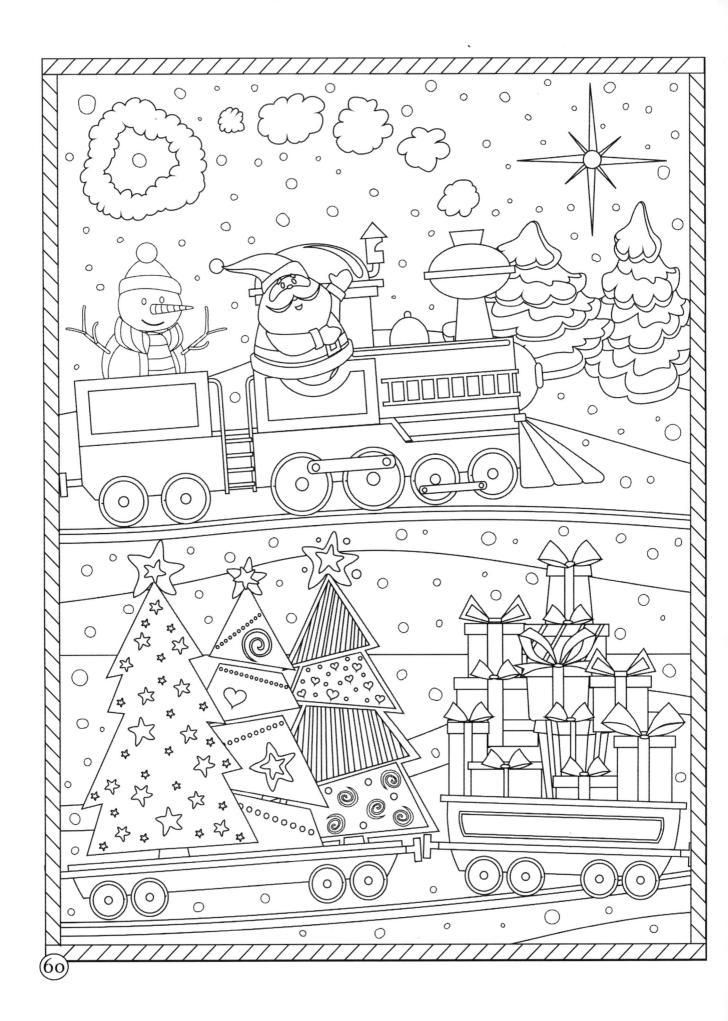

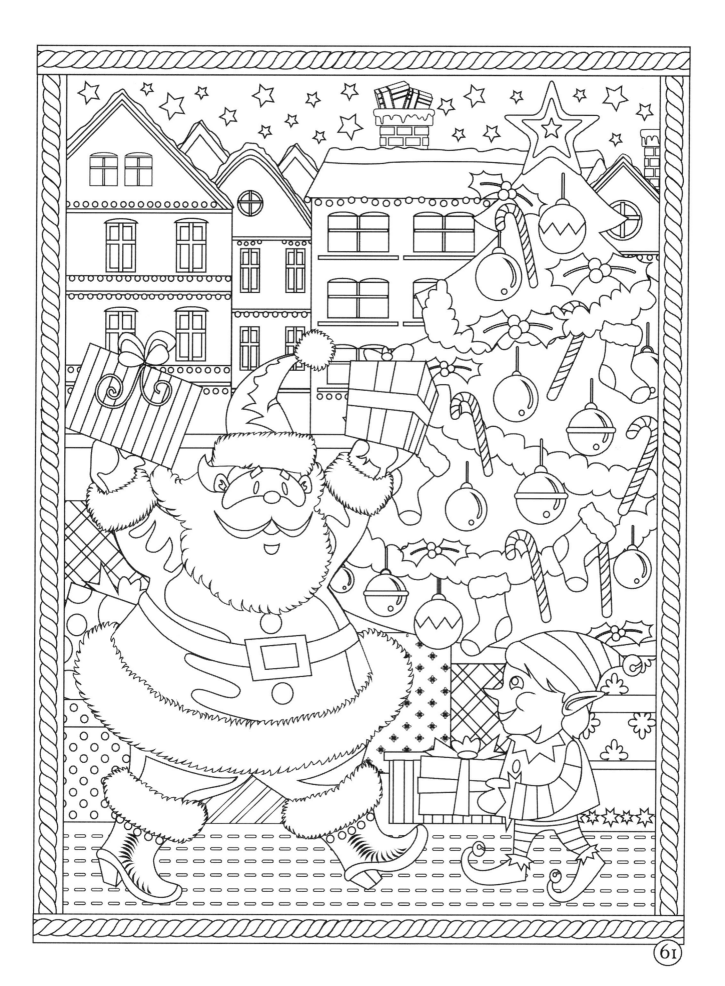

Blank page - helps avoid marker bleed-through!

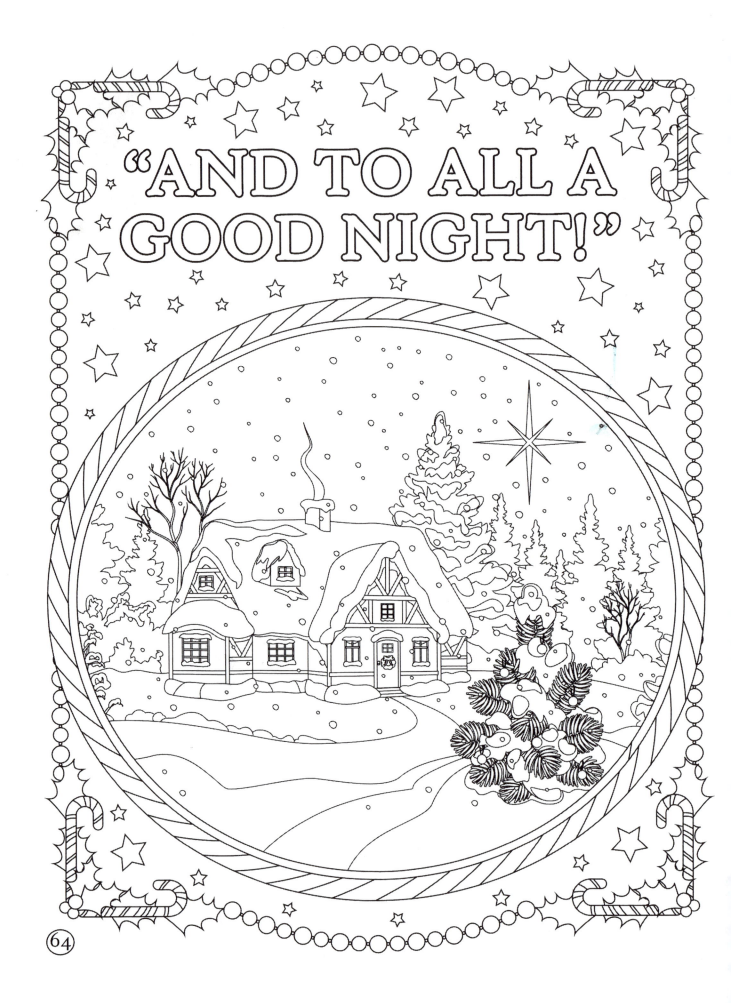